<u>Praise for *The 5th Inning*</u>

"Traditionally, it's viewed as a female occupation, to strip away the layers and examine the experience of relationships with a partner, with children, within one's own interior emotional life. Here comes a strong, real male voice, exploring the terrifying territory of growing older—in a marriage, in a family, in one's body. Ethelbert Miller writes with naked honesty and courage about what it is to be a man no longer young. Youth may have left him. Passion has not."
—Joyce Maynard, author of *At Home in the World*

"Poet and literary activist E. Ethelbert Miller's new memoir *The 5th Inning* is now available. Simply put, it's beautiful."
—Joseph Ross, American University

"It's clear that baseball is Miller's religion and the organizing metaphor for his life: 'Balls and strikes can also stand for BS. How much is thrown at a person by the time they reach 50?'"
—Jonetta Rose Barras, *Washington Examiner*

"Miller is not afraid to display his frailties, his misgivings about the time spent with his son and daughter, and his own strained relationships with his mother, father, and brother. He is open about his failures and asks how do we cope with failure in career, marriage, and life and how do we look at ourselves when we believe that we have failed as lovers, parents, and friends?"
—Brenda M. Greene, *Neworld Review*

"Beautifully written, every sentence is extremely well-crafted and labored over. Each sentence is another peek into the man's heart. Although *The 5th Inning* can sometimes be overbearingly sad, it's never depressing. So far, this is the best book I've read this year."
—Steve Hart, *Razorcake*

The 5th Inning

E. Ethelbert Miller

The 5th Inning
By E. Ethelbert Miller
ISBN: 978-1-60486-521-9
Library Of Congress Control Number: 2011939661
Copyright © 2012 E. Ethelbert Miller
This edition copyright © 2012 Busboys and Poets and PM Press
All Rights Reserved

PM Press
PO Box 23912
Oakland, CA 94623
www.pmpress.org

Busboys and Poets
2121 14th St NW
Washington, DC 20009
www.busboysandpoets.com

10 9 8 7 6 5 4 3 2 1

Layout and design: Josh MacPhee/Justseeds.org

Printed in the USA on recycled paper by the Employee
Owners of Thomson-Shore in Dexter, MI.
www.thomsonshore.com

Acknowledgements

I am deeply grateful to Andy Shallal and Busboys and Poets for making this book possible. Special thanks to the Virginia Center for the Creative Arts (VCCA) for providing me with a residency in May 2008. Without the time to write this book it would still be sitting in the dugout.

Thanks to Kirsten Porter, who served as editor and third base coach.

Much love to everyone who dreams of one day playing in the major leagues.

Let the poets sing the National Anthem.

May all our lives go into extra innings.

Dedicated to my wife, Denise King-Miller

The months and the years, a running river.
Then there's the day you wake up old.

Han Shan

(8th Century)

Dedicated to my wife, Denise King-Miller

The months and the years, a running river.
Then there's the day you wake up old.

Han Shan

(8th Century)

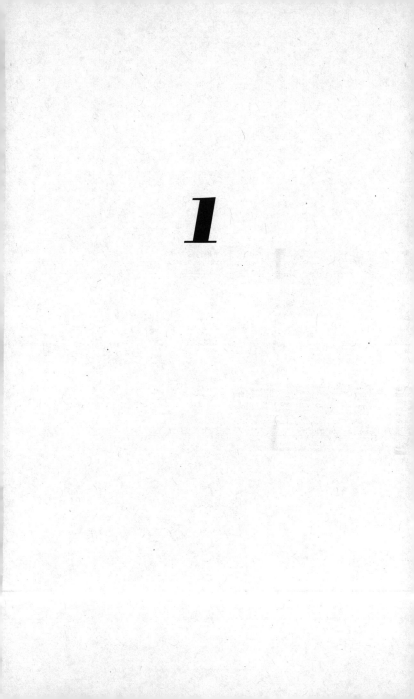

1

I DIDN'T WANT TO BECOME another Ellison. I had talked about writing a second memoir for several years. If I didn't begin immediately there would be no beginning. Whereas Ellison could never produce another *Invisible Man*, I wanted to surpass what I had done in *Fathering Words: The Making of an African American Writer*. The book was written as a tribute to the lives of Egberto and Richard Miller, my father and brother. Two black men who should have lived much longer and accomplished much more. *Fathering Words* was also about how I became a writer. For much of my life I have taken the poet's journey, the path which emanates from the heart. This rugged terrain has known tears, loneliness, and depression. Why continue to wear a mask? My first memoir featured two voices instead of one. I wrote in my sister Marie's voice and my own, creating a duet within the text. How could I tell my family stories when there were so many secrets kept from me? The curse of being the baby of the family. My sister, five years older, had a head full of hair and stories, too.

I wrote a good memoir published in 2000; the finished project surprised me like Jackie Robinson stealing home in front of Yogi. How could I find so many words to describe my path? I said silent prayers hoping the book would have a long life. Maybe a few were answered.

But now I'm pushing myself to write this second memoir. This book is a riff on middle-age, marriage, fatherhood, and failure. In baseball the fifth inning can represent a complete game. The structure of this book consists of balls and strikes. As a writer I might now and then throw the reader a curve. Balls and strikes can also stand for BS. How much is thrown at a person by the time they reach 50? When BS becomes just B, it might represent not balls but the blues. Four balls is a walk. The blues seen as departure and loss? The B also stands for blackness, perhaps the essence of the blues.

When August Wilson died at 60, I thought of the long conversation I once had with the novelist Charles Johnson a few months before Wilson went public with his illness. Charles had called me at Bennington College, where I was teaching creative writing. He told me Wilson was going to die. We were both angry and sad. Our long conversation became a lifeline for us both. We thought of how quickly life is suddenly over – so much work left undone. We are born with blank pages. Notebooks without lines. August Wilson seemed blessed because he was able to complete his cycle of plays prior to his death. But what about the majority of us? Our lives are often incomplete. We struggle to love like Wilson's character Citizen in *Gem of the Ocean*. By the time we turn 50 our bodies begin to fail. Mirrors might catch a glimpse of an aging body on the way to work and mumble some words in its direction. Maybe the mirror says "loser."

How do we cope with failure in life? How do we live when every day we open our eyes to death? This memoir is about how I coped with failure and disappointment in career, marriage, and life. We fail as lovers, parents, and friends.

It's almost the end of the fifth inning, and someone is getting up either in the dugout or bullpen. It's almost over, I tell myself. Why else write a book? Some of us fail as writers, too.

Baseball is still the American Pastime.

There is an inning in which husbands stop talking to their wives. It might be an argument that changes the score, taking love with it. How did I become one of those silent men sitting across the table from a woman with graying hair and a body now entering fall? When did my vows become autumn?

Love is difficult these days. Isn't it? I'm writing during a time of war. Yes, I thought my mission was accomplished after writing one memoir, but here I am acknowledging the past again. Yes, this might be another attempt at forgetting. Why try to remember? Why construct a memorial with words?

I'm often engulfed in loneliness. The nakedness of standing on the pitching mound alone. I've been crying too much. A sign of depression or sensitivity? One day I just couldn't take it anymore. My daughter was in the bathroom showering; my son was a cell phone call away. It was a film noir moment. Shadows, cigarette smoke, and a crazy dame. How do fathers handle disagreements with mothers? I wanted to walk out of the house with my blues. I couldn't keep fighting anymore. What terrorists' secrets had been kept from me? How did my life become Iraq? Why do I keep taking my shoes off when I enter the house? Can a home begin to resemble an airport before a ticket is checked? In my life I've witnessed too many good friends killing themselves as if they were workshopping a poem, novel, or memoir. What created those long sentences that ran out of air trying to explain the heart?

When a person becomes 50 or approaches the years that follow, his story is almost over. He can turn around and see the narrative he created. It might be about children, wealth, or personal achievements. The narrative is the story you find yourself in but can't determine if you're the author. You tell a woman you love her but its false intelligence. So much of this lately – so you apologize during this age of apology. How difficult can it be when so many others are apologizing for murder, war, adultery, and slavery? What is the difference between a confession and an apology?

What does a person confess after an error? A woman tells a man that marrying him was the worst mistake she ever made in her life. Is she confessing? Should he apologize?

So, I'm writing this memoir while sitting in a studio at the Virginia Center for the Creative Arts (VCCA). I've written five, six, maybe seven pages on my first day. I feel good. Discipline. Control. The narrative finding the corner of the plate. I have a postcard of James Baldwin on my desk. He is leaning against the pen and pencil holder. It's the photograph Jill Krementz took in 1973. Baldwin is wearing a shirt with a large collar. He has on a tie. He is 49. He isn't looking angry or mourning Malcolm or Martin. In this picture Baldwin is Miles. The coolness reflected in his stare into the camera. Into life. I remember in the early 1980s, being on the same program with Baldwin. We were at the Howard University Law School. I read a few poems first as if I was an early warm-up act for Aretha. Baldwin followed, lifting my words into his own and turning them into not just poetry but jewels. He spoke about his life as if he was Martin in Memphis. That point of not simply looking back but instead coming to that moment of measurement and truth. That moment when you know the price of the ticket but you have no cash. You turn around looking for someone to help you. You have an apology in one hand and a confession in the other.

2

THE INTRUDERS ARE SINGING, "Love is just like a baseball game. Three strikes you're out." I'm missing the second pitch. I'm in mid-swing about to hear the ball pop into the catcher's mitt. I'm waiting for it like that second shoe about to fall or the way Americans walked around after 9/11. Some of us are afraid. Afraid to say something isn't working. Well, maybe we're just afraid to say the whole damn thing is broken. You can't fix the economy or stop racism. You can't love another human being without failing.

Everything comes down to balls and strikes. You don't need religion or God to understand this. One can keep a scorecard just like God. Now and then you try to slow things down by stepping out of the box. I like how good hitters step back, adjust their uniforms, stroke their bats, survey the field, spit, grab themselves between the legs, step back into the box, touch their caps, stare at the pitcher, swing the bat a few times, and maybe if you're Ricky Henderson, step back out of the box and do it all over again. Balls and strikes. You can swing or take them. You can stand in the batter's box waiting for your pitch and never get it. Some people never learn how to hit. Anybody can get lucky if they can lay the bat on the ball. Political leaders try to be first ball hitters. Great jazz musicians can swing all the time. Rumor has it that the first slave in America got hit in the head with a pitch. A curveball?

I'm writing this memoir consisting of balls and strikes. Words changing into sliders, knuckleballs, forkballs, fastballs, and change-ups. I'm throwing sentences and paragraphs at readers. Hit this. Don't go chasing meaning where there is none. Some pitchers worry about their arms. I know it might be my kidneys or heart. My blood pressure is high so I keep checking my body for signs.

I read the obituaries every day and wonder what people will say about me. I expect the title "literary activist and poet" to be in the headline. Then there will be a reference to Howard University or the city of Washington. By the second paragraph there will be an attempt to determine the significance of my life. It's here that an entire career can be reduced down to one poem or book. If you're fortunate it could be the work that made you famous. Find a mistake in your obituary and you'll carry it to your grave.

How often has my name been misspelled? Will someone leave out the E? Will I be Ethelbert E. Miller throughout eternity? Will they mention Michelle, my first wife? Will they remember the women who I lived with? What about the women I only slept with once?

Maybe there will be a list of countries that I visited and then back to a few quotes from people who will claim they visited me – during the time I was hungry and it was their world.

Finally, one or two lines listing survivors; family members who maybe watched my coffin from the good seats.

John Madden is big on ceremonial bunting at big games. It's like having good polished shoes before you start walking. I haven't spent time thinking about where I would like to be buried or who would give my eulogy. Maybe I should. I hope it's not someone who only knew my work. Can you imagine Jesse Jackson or Al Sharpton speaking as if they knew me? Both of them probably stumbling over the correct pronunciation of my name. "Edlebert," my friend Jina says with her sweet Dominican accent. Her voice reminds me that I should have surrounded my life with more water. Be an island like so many of the members of my family that came from islands. West Indians. Bajans. But I imagine in my obituary nothing will link me to this geographical space and place. Why? Who destroyed the narrative? Where are the bones of my sins?

The words "literary activist and poet" seem to leave my lips very quickly when I'm asked to define myself. Is this a self-created identity? I started using the term around 2000. How come I find myself hesitating to describe myself as a father? Hasn't fatherhood been at the center of every decision I made or did not make over the last thirty years? Won't the last lines of my obituary mention my children's names?

Extra-innings. That's what one hopes for when the game seems to be ending. Doris Grumbach once wrote a memoir by this title. It's something I haven't thought about. My son and daughter seem to be living such different lives from my own. Yet what did my father think of me when my head was always in a book? We never played baseball in a park. I wonder if I'm as distant from my children as they are to me. My days of early fatherhood seem so much a blur these days. I associate family memories with places where I've lived in Washington. Is this what one calls making a home?

The Newport West, located at 1415 Rhode Island Avenue, is where I brought my daughter home after her birth. When I first moved into this apartment building the lobby had an upscale Bobby Brown look. The furniture in the lobby was missing a do-rag and the walls were red. A long time ago, one passed The Newport West and believed people with money lived there. Not true. One apartment was owned by prostitutes. Other units on my floor had doors I never saw open. I owned a duplex – split level. Two floors. The Newport West was an impressive place to live if you didn't want to impress anyone.

The day before my daughter came home, the place had no hot water. I had a pile of dirty dishes in the sink. I was a new father in a kitchen mess like the star on one of those bad comedy television shows. Maybe I would have a silly name like EE and every time something dumb would happen, an angry woman would scream: "Enough EE enough."

Fatherhood immediately made me confrontational. It was as if I had pushed aside King's "Letter from a Birmingham Jail" and wanted everything to be right for my new baby girl. Fatherhood consisted of moments of assemblage: car seat, crib, and toys. Not being good with tools or reading directions in several languages, I was hopeless at times. I detected disgust in my wife's eyes similar to a fan watching a relief pitcher blow a save.

My son was born when I lived at 1651 Fuller Street, NW. This building was owned by the art patron Herb White. It was a small white building with four floors pushed back from a street behind Columbia Road. It had a veranda instead of a terrace, and on the hot days you could watch all the drug transactions. If someone had told me there was a "God of Gentrification" I would have been on my knees almost every day and praying to it. How many fathers are forced to raise their children on Fuller Streets? It was a street my son would never play on. The father protects his herd, even though one night it was my cat Holly that probably saved our lives. One hot summer night before going to sleep, I checked in on my son and daughter sleeping in their bunk beds. They must have been eight and thirteen. My night ritual was to make sure to check on them. Rookies do that after their first hit. New to first base they look over at the first base coach. Didn't someone do the same for me? In my children's room was an unread *USA Today*. I had instructed them both to read the newspaper on a daily basis. Tonight the paper was folded and could have been left already prepared to swat bugs. I picked it up and decided to glance at a few stories before retiring. While reading in the outer room I noticed Holly my cat adopt an attack posture near the kitchen door. When I went to check to see what the problem was, I was shocked to discover a foot trying to push itself through my kitchen window. I yelled at the foot, and the foot took off. A few days later the police shot a person trying to climb into a neighbor's window.

It was not the foot but rather the bunk beds in the previous paragraph that encouraged me to purchase a house at 1411 Underwood Street, NW. Once known as being near the "Gold Coast," the five bedroom house saved my daughter's sanity. She felt that entering high school and still sharing a bunk bed with her brother was psychologically damaging. A family of four, we needed more space as much as Woody Allen needed the eggs.

DID YOUR DADDY EVER LISTEN to the blues or did he listen to himself?

Maybe a literary critic years from now will ask my children this question. I've been listening to the blues more than ever. Etta James? I never listened to Etta James before marriage. I did recall Thulani Davis mentioning her in a poem many years ago. Maybe the name got caught in the crease of my soul. I was trying to keep my mind straight, but the blues knocked me down. I took comfort in Ella's voice. Her songs touching my head, pressing my spirit against the wall. The blues find their way to your door on those days and nights when you simply don't talk to the person you live with. It's what some folks call being civil. Instead of yelling and throwing things and waking up neighbors, you keep the disagreements under water like you're drowning them until your own voice is gasping for air.

Small problems can create big arguments and days of silence between two people. You start believing those stereotypes about black women. You don't want to believe them but you do. It's why you find those black romance novels in the bookstores to be nothing but comic books. You listen to Etta James and decide it's not worth it to divorce and date again. The blues are a married man's Buddhism. I accept what God has given me, and sometimes I think he created me in my father's image. A black man sitting in a room talking to himself. Did DuBois call this chanting or just sorrow songs?

So much begins and ends on Underwood Street. Percival Everett's main character in *Erasure* lived on Underwood Street. A narrative similar to my own. Fiction? Not really. In *Things Fall Apart*, Achebe reminds us that all the stories are true. I could be Suder or Bud Powell. A man must be crazy to write poems and play jazz. How many words or notes can you keep in your head at one time? Fatherhood consists of how many notes? What sound is made when a father walks away? My mother once told me that my father's favorite song was "As Time Goes By." But was it the music or the movie? Did my father watch his dream get on an airplane? A tear falls down a woman's face and he's not there to catch it.

What would baseball be like without fans? A writer needs an audience. Here is what critic and scholar Julia Galbus has to say:

On a cold night in April, E. Ethelbert Miller gave a mesmerizing reading at the university where I teach. Afterward, I bought the last copy of Fathering Words *and asked him to sign it. I rarely asked authors to sign their books. It used to make me shy. Maybe I wanted an excuse to talk to him. I introduced myself and he responded, "You must be an administrator." What was I supposed to say to that? Afterward, the English department took him out for the customary meal at a German pub. Ethelbert was at one end of a long table eating a basket of fried catfish that made him queasy later. I was at the other end. As the beer started to take effect, one of the writers I teach with pointed out to Ethelbert that our department chair was black, as was our composition director, and wasn't that cool? Both women were present. I wanted to sink into the floor. The catfish was cold. Ethelbert migrated down to me and Jill (Kinkade). The dinner was winding down. Jill suggested we blow the joint. The three of us had tea at her house and she read his tarot cards. Dark symbols, most of them, surrounding a glowing heart. Portent.*

When do you stop reading horoscopes or simply accept the cards handed to you? How many times can you avoid death? When do you stop thinking about it?

I know I'm dying because so many of my friends are dying. It's the definition of friends that I keep in a jar next to the one marked acquaintances. The friends that are dying are the people I recognize mainly by face. I know the names of a few of them. They might be a person working in the post office, the father of a child in my son's class at school, or the woman who hands me pastries with plastic gloves in the supermarket. These people have become my friends only because we are friendly with each other. We live in a big city and we still speak. We care enough to have a conversation, offer a smile, a handshake, and a "good morning." When this is interrupted by death, we experience the coldness coming through an open window after a long summer. Death is the sudden draft on the back of one's neck. Who left the window open?

Cold. That is how I felt when I entered the post office at Howard University and found a flyer on a counter informing me of a memorial service for a woman I had recently purchased stamps from. How could she be dead? I was just talking with her a few days ago. You stare at the flyer, which has been poorly Xeroxed. Despite all the technology and new ways of printing, Black people still don't Xerox well. Some of our flyers and posters have that runaway slave look. We should just go with sketches. I read the flyer and know I'm not going to the memorial service. It's being held in some part of Maryland that I've never heard of and where people are still hunting for Frederick Douglass.

Death is like one of those hesitation pitches mastered by players in the old Negro Baseball League. A woman has her hand out to give you a few stamps and change back – and someone moans, "it's cancer." All your life it's been cancer. Even when everyone in your family was dying from heart attacks, you knew that everything bad was associated with cancer. You never studied it in school. It was never on your exams. Tumor. You know the word but have no idea what it looks like.

It's years ago and you're a child listening to your mother on the phone, and all of a sudden she says, "Yes, they opened her but there was nothing the doctor could do but close her back up. The cancer has spread too far." You did this when you spilled something in your briefcase or backpack. You look inside and see the mess. You just close it back up because you really don't want to deal with it or maybe you can't. Cancer. You think about it like the bad boys down the street. Will they leave you alone if you're nice to them? You disguise yourself with a walk that shows courage and maybe you begin to exercise and eat properly. But you know it might not work. You hear about another friend who is fighting cancer. It's breast cancer and maybe you dated this woman and you remember her breasts. They were beautiful and you held them as if they would melt in your hands or mouth. The softness was where you wanted to rest your head and forget about things.

Now you understand what those older black men at funerals were thinking. Here you are in a dark suit standing in front of a church or funeral home. You make small talk with someone you will never talk to again. The only thing you have in common is a relationship with the person in the coffin. After the funeral you won't have any reason to call one another. The business card someone hands you will be found in your suit pocket the next time you put it on. This could be months from now. You'll hold the card in your hand trying to place a face with it, but you can't. So you tear it in half and toss it in the garbage, the way a doctor might discard a lump of cells just taken from your lungs or head.

I'm counting blessings. I could be next. I can feel my body changing. The end of my season? The trading of a jersey for a hospital gown? If you take care of yourself people will be amazed by how good you look with your gray hair. Someone might ask about your diet or mention how you don't look your age. But you know your age. You're more aware of it each year or when you complete an application. There are fewer boxes to check where it says list age. How many people become angry when they discover they have been living in a box?

My friend Adrienne Black constructed my website and blog. I didn't know how many people were reading my E-Notes (blog) until we started tracking. The E-Notes in this book are similar to the ads you see around ball parks. They keep changing, creating another narrative, a duet with the scoreboard. I started writing E-Notes in 2004. Maybe there is no need to write a second memoir – just see E-Notes?

No. Here I am cutting and pasting. I'm leaving out the dates so the chronology resembles Cecil Taylor playing the piano.

E-Note:

I WATCHED THE FILM "UNFORGIVEABLE BLACKNESS" AND WAS KNOCKED DOWN BY JACK JOHNSON'S REMARK ABOUT WHY WHITE WOMEN WERE ATTRACTED TO BLACK MEN. JOHNSON'S COMMENT WAS "WE EAT COLD EELS AND THINK DISTANT

THOUGHTS." I FOUND THIS STATEMENT TO BE A VERY MODERNIST RESPONSE. IT HAS A STEIN POETIC QUALITY. JOHNSON WAS A NEW NEGRO AS MUCH AS JEAN TOOMER. JOHNSON'S RESPONSE IS SEXUAL, MYSTICAL, PERSONAL AND PROFOUND. THE DEFINITION OF SOUL (Blackness) HAS A DIRECT RELATIONSHIP TO THINKING DISTANT THOUGHTS. I LIKE HOW ELASTIC THE LINE IS. IT LINKS THE EXOTIC WITH THE MIND. THE MAN HAD "TASTE" WHICH IS WHY HE WAS ALWAYS COOL – EVEN IN THE RING. JACK JOHNSON CHANGED THE WORLD AS THE WORLD WAS CHANGING. NOT TOO MANY PEOPLE CAN DO THAT. ATLAS COULD ONLY HOLD IT UP.

People pay for what they do, and still more for what they have allowed themselves to become. And they pay for it simply: by the lives they lead.

– James Baldwin

MANY PEOPLE LIE when they check the box. They lie about their age. They lie about their health. I've always been curious about women who enter hospitals and never tell you what's wrong. It's always something personal they can't discuss. I try to block out sickness and death. I pull my cap down like a hard throwing reliever. But bad news is often the next batter.

I was in my room at Bennington College in Vermont when my wife called and told me about June Jordan's death. I waited a few moments for God to remove his hand from my chest. After my wife's call, there were a few calls from the media. I declined writing an appreciation for a major newspaper. I left my room and walked across the campus to the library.

The computer with its email has replaced the early morning phone call. How many times as a child did I hear the telephone ring around 3 am. Hiding beneath the covers I wondered if it was a wrong number. Let the bad news be for adults.

You pick up the phone in the dark. You can't see but you can hear. Sobs disguise the voice you're connected to by blood. It could be your cousin, aunt, or uncle. It could be somebody close but not too close to you. Maybe a person you don't talk too much to. You have a box of Christmas cards and you've addressed all, except one. You decide to send it to the person who is now talking on the phone. You send it to the person only after you've searched to find their correct address. When you were a child you would call out for help from your mother. She would be annoyed by your ignorance. "Boy, why you bothering me with such foolishness – don't you know where your auntie live?

No, I don't. I sit in front of the computer and type a few letters to people who knew June. I don't have details about her death. How much do you need to know about death? It's the memories of life that bloom into memoir.

I remember June and I sitting in a hotel lobby in Arizona at an annual Associated Writing Program Conference. We talked about publishing the letters we had written to each other beginning in the late 1970s. Laughing and being silly in our heads, we thought about a book that would be a commentary on black love. But all I have today are letters. A game ends after too many tears have fallen.

I didn't want to know the details about Reetika Vazirani's suicide or Liam Rector's suicide. They were close friends who lived in the next room. When you hear about suicide you punch the walls. You don't care about the physical pain that might mean your own broken bone. You want to break bones. Crush everything in sight. How could they leave you here alone? Liam had hired me to teach at Bennington. He was a culture warrior, a rogue and bard, a medieval man of letters. We sat once in his New York apartment surrounded by books, talking about literature and life, until the lights around the entire city came on. He told me it was time to walk the dog and so we went outside into the air and the sounds of traffic. Coming back into his building (after walking the dog only 5 sidewalk squares), Liam recounted the story of how one night a black guy rushed up to him in the streets and said, "Hey – don't you know me?" Liam said, "No." The guy tried to refresh his memory by saying, "Just think of your best black friend." Liam said "Ethelbert." "Right," the guy responded. "I'm Ethelbert's brother and I need a couple of dollars to get uptown." Opening his wallet, Liam gave the guy several dollars. It was on the elevator in his building that he realized he had been hustled. Liam was pissed. He knew my brother had died many years ago. He was still pissed as he stood in the doorway of his apartment telling me about the incident. Laughing, and laughing, I caught my breath and said, "Liam, you're only telling me this because you want your money back."

Loose change and memories. Liam. Liam. Liam. We talked about Reetika's suicide in the Commons at Bennington. The two of us framed by the window that looked out across the Bennington campus at what students called the end of the world. Knowing about my own depression, he asked if I was happy working in the writing program. I confessed and told him no. I looked at him and said, "If I'm standing here talking to you about five years from now – I'll kill you." He chuckled and nodded his head. "I'm serious, Liam." It was the last thing I said before going upstairs to dinner. I looked over my shoulder and saw a guy who had been hustled again. We suffer and pay too much when we lose close friends to suicide.

It's not the price of the ticket. It's opening your hand and finding only a stub.

Life is the art of hitting or pitching. You have to learn how to master one or the other. You're either in control or trying to gain control. Who needed steroids more, Barry Bonds or Roger Clemens?

Relief pitchers have short memories. They can quickly place success or failure in the past. They move forward or are removed. That's how I left the Bennington Writing Seminars. I decided to stop teaching before someone came for the ball. Wherever you work, pay attention to memos, outside consultant reports, and rumors that begin in the mail room. If you're in a job be looking for a new job. It's better to be a free agent instead of a bench player whose name is constantly mentioned in trade discussions. The bullpen is where I find myself struggling to get back into the starting rotation. It takes dedication and commitment. If you don't do it, middle age becomes old age and then you're living memories outside the casket at your own funeral.

The 5th Inning

Since baseball time is measured only in outs, all you have to do to succeed utterly; keep hitting, keep the rally alive, and you have defeated time. You remain forever young.

– Roger Angell

6

ONE THING I HAVE ENJOYED in my life has been watching my son play basketball. I was never good at the game. One day my father picked up the one basketball in our house and took it outside. I went with him. We were living in the St. Mary's Projects in the South Bronx. It was Sunday and the basketball courts were empty. For about twenty minutes my father looked like an idiot trying to shoot or dribble. He had no idea of how to play. It was just me, my father, and the ball. We would never again share another moment like this.

My father taught me a lesson that day. He taught me how a man needed to take a break from the sadness in his life. He couldn't teach his son something he didn't know. My father was a failure at sports; yet for a brief moment it didn't matter, because he looked over at me and passed the ball.

Nyere is shooting over my outstretched hands. It's a Sunday and we are at Ft. Stevens Park. I'm winded. My son is laughing and talking trash. I can't stop him from scoring and he knows it. I'm at that point in fatherhood when your child no longer has to listen to you. If you've raised a good child – just count the basket. Two points. I think about this as my son and I walk back home – the space between us the size of love. He flips the ball in my direction. I know he can play with the best of them, but what did he ever learn from me?

I believed until now that all things of the universe were, inevitably, fathers or children. But behold that my pain today is neither father nor child.

– Cesar Vallejo

My daughter, Jasmine-Simone, is close to me but she's closer to her mother. What does this mean? How do I feel? Maybe your first-born child should be closer to the womb than the others that emerge. What does closeness mean? It's the sound of voices laughing in the next room, especially the kitchen. When you enter the room the conversation stops or a chair moves and space is made for you. But you don't fit. Your knees stick out and when you look at everyone the subject of the conversation changes or your wife says, "Do you want something to eat?"

Sometimes it's me and my daughter on a bus looking at people. I know we are related because when something funny happens, we don't need to look at each other – and there is always begging in my daughter's eyes. They say, "Daddy, please don't laugh because if you do, I won't be able to stop either." It's during these moments that I don't think about asking her about her personal life or who she is dating. I love her for the person she is. There is a section of my daughter's bone marrow that's conservative. At times I think I'm talking with a distant West Indian relative in Brooklyn. My daughter is sorrel and plantains. She is rice and peas and sweet bread. She's my seashell buddy. All this flows in her blood and she can morph into my mom as quick as a computer click. My daughter believes strongly in family. But what if the Liberty Bell has a crack?

Hey dad, it's hard to think of just a list of things that I've learned from you over the years. Mostly because I'm still growing and still learning. But I think you have most influenced my passion for learning and have encouraged me to be a leader. My love for current events and reading the newspaper started because you used to quiz me and Nyere on current events during dinner and make us watch Dan Rather in the evening. I have always thought that my father is the smartest person I know, and each day I strive to be a little more like you – read a little more…maybe an entire newspaper.

You encouraged me to be a leader even though I was very shy as a child. I remember being in high school and you told me I should run for school president, but I settled on class representative. It's taken a while for the encouragement to sink in, but I'm slowly taking on more leadership positions as I get older. I also learned sports from you. Remember when you used to wake me and Nyere up at 6 AM to play basketball and football?

When I'm very ill or dying, I can see my daughter coming to the hospital to visit. I can see the patient in the next bed turning on his side and saying, "You're blessed to have a beautiful child who still cares about you." I'm not sad that we all have to die one day; I'm sad that so many of us will die alone. We will depart from the earth with our children living in another city. Maybe on a small desk or table there will be a card and flowers and maybe the phone will ring once a week. Maybe the grandchildren will send pictures drawn in crayon, adding a few misspelled words. You will prop yourself up in the bed and hold either a pill or a memory in your shaking hand. You will turn to stare at the ceiling or walls. The tasteless food will be cold on a tray.

7

DENISE HAS BEEN TO THE CVS three times in one day. She has finally spoken to the store's manager. They have given me the wrong medication. If I had taken the stuff, this book would have ended before it started.

"When A Man Loves A Woman" is the song we decided to play at our wedding back in 1986. It's one of those songs that you can't forget the first few lines or notes to. It's also one of those songs you wish you knew all the words to. I hear it echoing in my head whenever my wife and I have an argument.

In the kitchen her back is to me. Is it my mother's back? She's cooking and not listening. Oh, if food had ears I wonder what it would hear? When she turns around I see the expression that introduced many black men to hats. There are perhaps Einstein equations that prove the speed of light can never alter nor change a physical body if it remains married to the same person for almost thirty years. Or what makes a baseball curve?

Love defies physics and that's why Denise and I are still living together. Now and then a player looks at the standings or maybe across the field into another dugout. What would it be like to play in Fenway or Yankee Stadium? Curt Flood pulls divorce papers from the drawer. It's the top of the fifth inning and you dream about the romance that can surprise even history in the ninth. But what if the game ends in the 5th inning? How many ways can a poet die?

Julia Galbus sends me a note:

If the book is mainly dark (and games that get called in the 5th inning for weather are dark), what is the light that keeps you going, what sparks balance the despair?

So you catch yourself in mid-sentence not wanting to argue anymore. In mid-sentence you think about a divorce or maybe just putting on the coat with the hood in the back of the closet. You left it there after the last snow fell. You didn't want to put it on then but you did. It's the same thing with your old pair of sneakers. Because you don't have boots you wear sneakers in the snow. You slip and glide your way to the corner to get a newspaper. You're not going to work. No one in your neighborhood is even out. Folks are sleeping through a storm. No cars. No bus. Just your own footprints leading back to your house. You retrace them and realize you're going to have to come back out and clean the steps, the walkway, and in front of the building. You don't want to do this. You hate the snow and the gray cold that returns every winter, but then didn't you get up this morning and look at your wife? You listened to her snoring. The sound of something humming in the kitchen. You want to adjust the flame but you can't. The bed is a stove without fire. A fool consumed with passion would run outside and stick his hands in the snow.

When you were a boy you didn't like matches. You never wanted to burn yourself. But look at you now? Blisters on your hands from your turn at bat. Your hands burning from a ball hitting the center pocket of a glove. How long have you been catching this game? I tip my cap when I come home. When did it replace the kiss?

Gravity. People discover it in their marriage as they become older. Why do things fall apart in a home? Is it because gravity is known to suck the air out of a room? Romance falls back to earth. Dreams collect dust. Wedding pictures stick together. Silence starts the next conversation. Pitchers balk and fans boo. The television camera catches a player sitting on the losing team with a big smile on his face. What's going on in his mind? What is he thinking? How many men try to smile their way into the arms of another woman? Gentle drops of rain? Rain falling. Nothing but rain. You're still out there on the mound, holding the ball, running your fingers down the seams of what might just be your family. Turn your back to the plate, the catcher, the umpire and watch the rain fall. Are you falling? It's the hard rain that beckons the ground crew, the obit writers and the gravediggers. It's the hard rain that pulls the trigger and slits the wrists. It's the hard rain that's going to fall.

THE 5TH INNING

In the middle of warming up you feel it.
Your catcher feels it too. He throws the ball back to you
a little harder, like a pat on your butt. You're both in the
bullpen but it could be a bedroom and you're like two
lovers knowing each other's moves. You place your hand
on the ball and feel the stitches. Your fingers remember
all the memories that flow from your arm. This day you
will remember as sudden as the curve which breaks and
begs for a hitter.

Just before the first pitch of the game you look for the
signal. Fastball. What else? You look away and then
back again. Fastball. When it leaves your arm it's fire
burning with prophecy. Every batter at this moment is
a believer. The umpire makes the call and the crowd
genuflects back into their seats. The game begins. The
catcher throws the ball back to you, and you turn and
look out at the centerfield wall. You check the score-
board and your eyes rest on the flag blowing in the

wind. Every batting order is a minefield. Any ball you throw can explode off a bat and be the reason for your defeat. By your third pitch you push this thought out of your mind. You break a curve over the plate and the batter's legs and arms never move. When you were a kid, this is how you stood when someone placed a gun to your head. You pleaded and cried for your life. You were helpless. You look over at the dugout and you catch a coach spitting at his feet. He knows you have it today. As the next two batters swing like ghosts trying to touch something real you think about how you could be Gibson or Koufax.

Three strikeouts and you move into the second inning and get two more. The third batter grounds out to the shortstop. The crack of the bat stuns the crowd and you realize you could throw like this forever.

You reach the bottom third of the batting order and you know you're facing three guys who believe you're God today. You decide not to rest and so you stay ahead in the count. Someone hits a foul ball and you learn how difficult perfection is. Still you've come this far and you feel good. The sweat under your shirt places a hand upon your heart.

The first batter up in the fourth inning is the leadoff hitter again. It's a movie sequel. Will it be as good as the original? You throw a soft change-up and he kisses the surprise with a bunt down the first base line. You run to catch the ball spinning on the grass and when your bare hand catches it you think of a woman who once seduced you in a hotel. You feel naked as the hitter places his foot on first base and he's safe. A bunt is a soft kiss off a bat, a rolling tongue or lip wet with desire and nothing else. Sometimes it just comes to a stop and there is nothing to do but pick it up and mutter something under your breath.

One runner on and another batter up. You pitch for the first time from the stretch position. Your eyes looking over your shoulder like a spy. Why take any risks. You play it safe and throw a fastball to the hitter. Out of the corner of your eye you catch the runner running. You know it's a hit and run before the bat hits the ball. There's nothing you can do. You're in trouble with players on first and third. You shake your head and realize what you were feeling in the bullpen was sugar. It was sunlight at the end of an afternoon. There's a bitter taste in your mouth. You feel cheated. It's bad luck. It's your arm failing you again. No, it's more than that. It's what love feels like when it's gone. When you look down a street or across a bed or wait for a door to open after a door has closed. Love is what you throw to the next batter and he's ready. The ball is long gone and you don't even turn around to look toward the fence. A homerun and three runs cross the plate. You tug your cap and pull at your pants and catch your breath. You settle down the way a man might move his ex-wife's things from a hallway closet. The next three outs come as easy as dating.

In the fifth inning you know anything can happen. This could be a complete game. You count your blessings for surviving the fourth. The first hitter sends a ball deep to the warning track in left field. This brings your manager to his feet. He starts to pace in the dugout. He's afraid you're losing it. You look down at your feet and kick the rubber. You're afraid too and it tips the next hitter off. One swing and you're down four. The next two hitters follow with a single and a double. It's over now. You might as well play catch in the backyard with the kids. The catcher asks the umpire for time and walks out to the mound. Here comes your manager getting ready to ask for the ball. Inside your glove you hold it and keep waiting for it to speak. The silence tells its own story. The game keeps searching for an author.

9

So what went wrong? Do you want to talk to the sports writer, therapist, or literary critic? Was it you or the other team? I feel like Gil Hodges when he played for the Mets. I wake up dreaming about the Kansas City Athletics and the Philadelphia Phillies. Baseball hell. For Denise it had to go downhill when we moved to Fuller Street. The wrong stadium for a woman from Iowa. I think she cried or cursed every time she walked down the street. Young drug pushers sitting on cars, women hanging out of windows screaming at children or cursing at men. It was pain without a curfew. A small street where I didn't get to know people until we moved. I bump into Darlene at the Howard University post office somewhere between one of these chapters. We embrace as if we are family. Darlene lived on Fuller and was known for her hips and butt. What was I known for? I was Herb White's colored friend who lived in the big white house with a wife and two kids. Now and then someone saw me on television and they were proud to live on Fuller Street. Insanity for the oppressed.

I can imagine Denise sitting in the apartment listening to the nonstop symphony of cursing and music spilling from cars and wondering what did she do to deserve this. Was this in her stars? It was on Fuller that she began to handle crystals and pursue the path of Divine Science. Was she bitter at me? Would I have to wait almost twenty years for Obama to provide an explanation? Small street. Small town. What's the difference?

A woman will find another road to salvation when the man she marries fails to provide. I was working at Howard University and making a little more than nothing. I had no wardrobe. No savings. Nothing but books. I was the Polo Grounds in need of Willie Mays. What did Denise ever see in me? I was an error in her life. I was a bad hop like the one that knocked Tony Kubek down. One day I looked at my wife's hand and she was wearing a wedding ring that I didn't recognize. I imagine it was something her mother gave her to avoid embarrassment. What conversation came with the ring? Could Lorraine Hansberry place words in their mouths?

The stadium is a stage. Denise looks at the scoreboard and decides to buy a house. This is the way out. The dream for family and sanity. The escape from the wretched of the earth.

For me the idea of home ownership was like playing in the majors. I never thought about it. I grew up in the South Bronx. The St. Mary's Projects was New Orleans before Katrina. I didn't know how to repair or fix anything. I had problems with hammers and screwdrivers. My solution to everything was either pull the plug or kick it again. What would I do in a home of my own? Where would Whitey Ford be in 1961 without Luis Arroyo? Who would be my lifesaver? Arroyo was the first Puerto Rican player to play for the New York Yankees. I can still see him making that long walk from the bullpen. His jacket hanging off one shoulder.

Denise. Dear Denise. The definition of Denise: Wife. Mother. Lifesaver? Denise saved me from the many female barracudas in DC. I have so many emotional scars. What does the E stand for in my name? Evidence. How many times was I hit in the head by a woman? Beanballs and sex — what's the difference? Which one is the worst headache?

When we moved from Fuller to Underwood my children had their own rooms. Everyone had a door. Who invented the door? Was it created to get out or stay in? What happens when doors come between people? I don't know how to drive, so I have to wait for my wife to open the door. It has always been this way.

One day I simply decided to stop and look at all the doors surrounding me. I caught myself knocking on a door. Was happiness on the other side? Knock. Knock.

Denise tells me to close the door to the bedroom.

On August 18, 1967 in Fenway Park, Jack Hamilton threw a ball that hit Tony Conigliaro. The young Boston Red Sox star suffered a broken cheekbone and damage to his left retina. A door began to close on a promising career. I was never a Red Sox fan. Growing up as a child in the South Bronx, I quickly became a Mantle and Maris boy. Me, a Yogi Berra, Elston Howard, Johnny Blanchard, Hector Lopez, Bobby Richardson type of guy. I loved the Yankees and wanted to inherit Clete Boyer's position at third base. I wanted to dive into the dirt and backhand hard hit grounders near the bag. I wanted to throw runners out from my knees. Baseball was my religion.

I didn't grow up hating the Boston Red Sox. Looking back on my childhood, maybe it was this team that introduced me to poetry. I just loved saying the names of the guys who played for them. Names like Carl Yastrzemski, Bill Monbouquette, Tony Conigliaro, and of course Pumpsie Green. Pumpsie. Yes, he was one of the first black players on the Red Sox. I had his baseball card. Pumpsie. A name as different as some folks find Ethelbert today.

It was just around the time that gentrification hit Washington that I began to see more white people around the city wearing Red Sox caps. A sign of things changing? It's impossible to write about one's own life without observing the other games and players. For instance, there seem to be many African-American poets these days. For every Starbucks on a corner one can find someone who went to the Cave Canem workshops. For every poet fathering words there are dozens sleeping with the dictionary. African-American poets playing the majors. Look for them to change the literary landscape with the work they produce and by teaching in creative writing programs. How many will win major awards? One applauds their success, but how will history remember someone like Ahmos Zu-Bolton? Didn't he once tell the story about pitching against Vida Blue? Zu might as well have played in the old Negro Baseball League. His name is now an answer in a trivia game. A few months before he died we spoke on the phone. He joked about how he was in the hospital fasting. Another attempt to create folklore out of sickness. I was half expecting him to say that Mama Easter had given him some hoo-doo medicine and advice to keep the poems coming back to him like women.

Ahmos Zu-Bolton's death was a slave ship coming into port. It was filled with too many mysteries and lies. What happened during the Middle Passage of his life? How did this guy survive? On what road in Mississippi or Louisiana did he sell his soul to the devil with a guitar? Here was a guy talking about science fiction poetry before the world discovered Delaney or Butler. A literary Sun Ra – but didn't Sun Ra write poems too?

I believe Ahmos made it beyond the fifth inning. No one was certain about the date of his birth. He must have turned a Satchel Paige. Ahmos Zu-Bolton and Liam Rector both worked for *Black Box Magazine* in the 1970s. Black Box. The two words such a description of my father's ashes and what was lowered into the ground of a Yonkers cemetery. The box once again. I keep checking on my friends and they keep descending into boxes. Tony Conigliaro died in Salem, Massachusetts, in 1990. He was 45. Salem. Witchcraft. HooDoo Hollerin and Bebop Ghosts.

At poetry readings I read the work of friends no longer here. I should start wearing a black armband. So many gone. Etta James is singing "Blue Gardenia" and I turn around on the mound and feel the passing breeze. The next pages are difficult to pitch.

I need to connect my life to others and see what pattern emerges. I can't be the only one walking around on this bitter earth feeling this blue. How did I get to be so black and blue? I could be Ellison listening to Armstrong. I could be back on the first page of this memoir again.

One Sunday I walked down the street to the store and purchased five composition notebooks. I had been reading a review of Arnold Rampersad's Ralph Ellison biography in The New Yorker. *I didn't want to become another Ellison.*

Another note from Julia Galbus:

Hi E,
I read your memoir. I think it has a lot of powerful mo-
ments. I don't think it's ready to send to an agent yet.
It's not clear to me what the structure is going to be, or
where it is headed with the metaphor. I think you should
just keep writing...

How many narratives have been changed by Iraq? I'm standing in front of a room full of soldiers on a military base in Italy. The young men and women have witnessed war in Iraq and Afghanistan. I'm trying to tell them how they can all write a memoir. How to begin. What to include and leave out. I'm telling them about the importance of storytelling. I'm trying to get them to see their lives from different perspectives. What's beyond the wartime experience? Peace?

It's strange looking at all these young soldiers and not seeing my own children. No wonder in the early days of the war some made wrong turns in their military vehicles and were never seen again. I was in Iraq in the 1980s. I was invited by the Iraqi government to attend a poetry festival. I walked around the streets of Baghdad and visited the holy mosque in Karbala and the ruins of Babylon. Iraq was at war with Iran, so missiles were often falling from the sky.

I grew up on World War II movies, a time when one was always waiting for an alarm or siren to go off. One was led down to a dark basement. Maybe after an hour of bombing, people would emerge unscathed from beneath the rubble. Smoke would be in the air but so would the smell of survival and eventually freedom. Life isn't like the movies so I was not prepared with the random suddenness of being "rocked" without warning. It made everything so random and unpredictable. I amused myself by thinking about my obituary. "Poet, born in the Bronx, is killed in Baghdad." Strange, I could not detect my future or the tragedy.

In baseball it might begin as simple as a walk. You find yourself on first base in another country. My father never got to see the world. He never flew on an airplane. Why have I been so fortunate? Why did I have a chance to visit Israel in 2004 and walk the streets of Jerusalem? This was a city I know my brother Richard would have given anything to see during his lifetime. My brother struggling to become a monk in the South Bronx. I thought about him when I was in Israel and Iraq. When I looked around at all the Sudanese workers helping to rebuild Babylon, I could hear my brother whispering into my ear. My brother who kept a picture of Haile Selassie on a wall in his apartment. While in Babylon, I was feeling Bob Marley's lyrics kissing my spirit. My brother's ghost swaying to my heartbeat.

When does a walk become the movement of Jah people? Maybe this is where the narrative becomes more than one voice crying in the wilderness. Whose memoir is this?

Who will tell the stories of young men and women killed in the Middle East? Who will remember the stories from New Orleans? What memories keep coughing up the images of the collapsing Twin Towers? What about the Tsunami? How fast can you run? No, you "walk" through these events because they don't directly affect you. You walk away. You keep walking. You even walk away from your own mother who heard the 9/11 planes pass her apartment window in Tribeca.

My mother lives south of Canal Street and her neighborhood was marked as the "frozen zone." My mother's hair is gray, the color of the endless smoke that seems to still rise from Ground Zero. A couple of nights I went to bed thinking about my mother and the rest of the world. In the media, folks were talking about life never being the same again, and one scholar talked about the "new normal."

I called my mother yesterday and asked how she was doing. She told me she was going outside for a walk. She sounded calm and normal. I wondered how she felt when she walked outside and turned the corner. Her eyes looking upward at the sky – her faith in God as strong as ever. A few blocks away, the Towers of man reduced to nothing; an entire civilization awaiting poets to step forth and describe the new.

How do I push aside the personal blues and begin to write about the Beloved Community? How can I find a voice to be uplifting if I can't uplift myself? Who is this stranger in the mirror? I walk around as if I was another refugee in the world.

So what's the problem? Where does the loneliness and depression come from? Inheritance? You think of your friends Beverly and Meri and how the shadows stole their wardrobes. Every morning a difficult morning to rise. Once I went over to Meri's apartment and pulled open the curtains. The sun can disappear behind the make-up a woman wears. I think of Beverly fleeing the Washington area almost every month. No telling where she might be. Russian roulette? The last time we corresponded she was in Argentina living on a secret a day. I look at a map and realize I can no longer navigate the oceans between our friendship. Meri keeps moving too. I lose track of so many of my friends between the writing of books.

I have several old phone books and a large box filled with business cards obtained over the years. I have no idea anymore who many of the people are. There are places in the phone books where I crossed out names and marked "deceased." I have a desire to take a pen or marker to my own name. It would be like jumping to the Metro tracks at the Takoma Station around 8 am. No one would be able to get to work on time. People would cuss loudly and gather on the platform. It would take thirty minutes for an ambulance to arrive and re-move my body. Folks coming up the escalator would inquire, "What's going on?" For maybe the first time in my life I might be able to let someone know.

THESE SHORT CHAPTERS ARE the equivalent to balls and strikes. If I write too many of them you know I'm having trouble trying to find the plate. That's how one's life can begin (or end). Several years of college and you still don't know what to do. Thirty years working in the same place and you wonder – why?

I once believed there would be a revolutionary change in the world. Even when I was reading books by Herman Kahn, I believed the future would be better. But I don't know now. Every day another natural disaster. Every day a man finds a new way to torture another man. When I was younger I read about nationalism and saw it as an essential first step to measure progress in a society. Today I see the limitations of nationalism and how ethnic suspicions can place a machete in a hand. As I grow older I can no longer espouse certain beliefs. It's difficult to read many of the books published by black intellectual pundits. I've been saved by the blog. Since 2004 I've written E-Notes. Do you want to know what I think? Read an E-Note. What better way to read my stats. They are all there waiting for a biographer to decipher. Baseball more than any other sport keeps a stat on everything. How many women have I dated that were not African Americans?

But can you trust the blog? How truthful are writers when they write for an audience? What might an E-Note tell you that this memoir won't? Why not just keep blogging?

The last few years I've taught a number of workshops on how to write a memoir. How to get started and how to finish. I've already written the ending of *The 5th Inning*. I could stop and let you read it right now. It begins:

> *He can only hold her for so long*
> *No one's home but the lights are on*
>
> *– Amy Winehouse*

Light rain falling. I look into the mirror at the gray. I'll be sixty soon. Will I make it? How many innings left? Denise is driving down from DC to take me home. But where is home? So many people around the world homeless. Refugees of the heart. I want to love again. See the old country one more time. Make love to Denise again? Hear the old language spoken...

The memoir writer has to decide what secrets not to tell. The memoirist writes not to harm or injure anyone with words. Keep healing and transformation of the self in the center of one's thoughts. Look at pictures of love ones. Visit the old neighborhood. Think of the sounds you miss. The smells you remember when you open a door. The words of Mark Doty help but there are many authors whose books can be blueprints. Lee Gutkind has his *Creative Nonfiction* journal. Now and then there are helpful tips in it. It's the craft you master that will introduce you to the big leagues. How many people are still unaware that I wrote *Fathering Words*? Should I discard this manuscript and return to poetry? Who is going to publish this? This isn't a sequel. If it was, I would have to include my sister's voice. What would she say?

It seems as if all the years of my life have been spent taking care of my mother. After the car accident in Brooklyn, I didn't know what was going on. We could all have died. There was my mother sitting in the car seat next to me. It's always me. My brother doesn't even know how to drive. What help is he? He is in Washington and sometimes I don't know where I am except maybe stuck in traffic between Manhattan and Yonkers. Is my life an accident? What happened to my marriage? Was that an accident too? My brother keeps talking about a fifth inning, but I passed that years ago. Big deal. Age is like the temperature outside. If you need to wear a sweater, wear one. I feel my best when I'm on a cruise in the Caribbean. I love the water as much as my father did. I love to surround myself with water. I would drown

if I was married again. Maybe that's the difference be-
tween my brother and me. I love being an island.

If I were an island I would be touched by water. A hand or wave on my chest or back. It would be
easier to cope. I would have sand and shells. I would
be known for my beaches and not my poetry. What kind
of trees would I have? Would I be able to comb clouds
from my hair? What about being an unknown island?
Who would discover me? Call me Puerto Rico and I
could dance with my friend Naomi Ayala. We could
speak Spanish in my forest. There would be magic hid-
den in my mountains. The island of my imagination has
no boundaries.

I think all memoirs should consist of magical
stories. How often did I imagine myself playing for the
Yankees when I was a child? It was I – and not Mickey
Mantle – who hit the home run in the bottom of the
ninth. We didn't call it a walk-off homerun back then.
We didn't stand in the batter's box like Reggie Jackson
or Manny looking at our art work. We didn't cast our
bats aside like fishing rods or spears. No, there was no
posturing or television highlight. We played the game
not like entertainers but like workers putting in a good
days work. We played with our backs hurting and our
hands bruised. We played with bad knees and sore
muscles. Some of us were iron men and others were
simply legends. Joe and Ted swinging bats. Willie putting things in a basket and Vic Power doing it all with
one hand.

I fell in love with baseball and lost my virginity to a glove. Gloves with names like Bobby Shantz and Elroy Face. How ironic to always be given a relief pitcher's glove. Once I had a glove with the name Nellie Fox on it. I would sit in a corner of a room punching my hand over and over again into the pocket. There were many days when I didn't have anyone to play with. One day a tomboy by the name of Judy took my glove, and took off running. I would see Judy years later, during my freshman week at Howard. She was now a community black militant shaking down black college kids for revolutionary dimes. I was 17 and didn't know a Fanon phony from a Malcolm X. I came to Howard University in 1968 and encountered my first rain delay. Thirty years later I need to compose a long poem like Cesaire's *Return to My Native Land*. How do I pay tribute to this island known as Ethelbert? Where was the game of baseball invented?

I have shown you the path to liberation.
You should understand that your liberation depends on
yourself.

– The Buddha

I THINK MY BROTHER RICHARD was trapped inside himself when he left the monastery in the early Sixties. How did it feel to undertake the journey from upstate New York back to the South Bronx? I can imagine my brother with his beautifully shaven head packing his belongings into one suitcase. Who took him to the air-port? What did the last monk tell him? What happens when an older brother returns from what was supposed to be his dream? How is he viewed in the eyes of his baby brother? My brother knew he had failed. It was because of his failure that he loved me with a deep love. The love of brothers. The reason for brotherhood.

A few months before his death he called me one morning. He was crying and he mentioned how he felt so alone. This telephone conversation became a wound and then a scar inside of me. It was something that made me afraid of myself. I knew exactly what my brother was feeling, and I was married at the time. My brother and I were born with holes in our hearts. Richard tried to fill the hole with his faith and also music. I turned to sports – first baseball and then football and basketball. But I was never really good at it. My mother never permitted me to play in the little league. It was my mother who also wrote the letters to my brother that eventually tugged or rather pulled him out of the monastery. My brother was like a pitcher who gets knocked out of the game before the first inning is even completed. It happens to young rookies and old veterans. They can't get the outs. Or maybe you're the batter and you see a big time curve for the first time. You see the ball coming directly at your head. You can't move, your legs are gone. You accept the fact that it's beanball time for you, but then the pitch breaks like a dish falling off a table and it's just a strike. You look down as the catcher looks up – smiling at you. Before he throws the ball back to the pitcher maybe he winks. It's either a welcome or subtle way of saying you're out of your league baby. You're holding the bat like someone's sweetheart. Maybe my brother had a moment like that while he was a monk. Maybe behind those Trappist walls of silence he began to hear his own voice. A voice that was limping and begging for help. My brother was in love with St. Francis and I was in love with my brother. His weeping soon became my own.

My brother disliked sports. I don't think he ever played the game or even knew the game was being played. We never sat and watched a ballgame together. We never played catch. My brother was always burning candles in his bedroom where he had built a small altar. I mentioned once in a poem — this is where my fear of fire probably started. Was I waiting for a candle to set fire to the curtains? What about possible burns to my skin?

But isn't following "the path" about the burning away of ego and desire? What about the flame of things? My brother dead before he reached fifty. My father sitting in a black limousine staring into his empty hands on the way to Richard's funeral. However Richard had died years before. He was buried in his failure. A few years after his death our father would be buried next to him.

When will I claim my inheritance? Or perhaps the future rests with my ability to reinvent myself. In my house on Underwood Street, there are several statues of the Buddha. The first one was given to me by my friend Don Mee Choi, another was received from Charles Rowell, and a third — the weeping Buddha — was a gift from Adrienne Black. A long time ago my father purchased a small laughing Buddha with a big belly. I didn't even know it was a Buddha. His belly resembled my father's body. Maybe this was a clue I never saw until now. Is this how the memoir pokes the writer in his side? A catcher throws a ball back to the pitcher — a bit harder — just to get his attention. He wants the pitcher to concentrate. I need to breathe and write more...

It's my second week at the Virginia Center for the Creative Arts. I'm writing well and it feels like I have two pitches working. If I can find a third pitch to throw, I'll be able to complete this book by the end of May 2008. Thirteen chapters of fastballs and curves. How about a slider or knuckleball? Do I dare?

Some people pick up a memoir and look for spice. How honest is the book? What secrets are being revealed? Show me the good parts. Name names. Another Black Sox scandal? Memoir as evidence?

A man meets a woman in a café. She has grace and charm. She could be new in town. She could know your superstitions. Are you afraid to step on the line or cross the line? When you embrace that first time, your lungs fill with perfume and just the scent of her seduces your fingertips and tells your toes to be careful – so you don't follow her to the door. Only your eyes do. You're Houdini and desire has pulled you underwater and there are locks and chains keeping you inside your life. How many years can you survive without air?

Was my daddy a magician? Why did he love the theme song to *Casablanca*? You follow a woman up the stairs to her apartment. At the door you have to take off your shoes. You're so mesmerized by her beauty that you remove your socks too. The floor meets your nakedness and you decide this is all you need tonight. You look around at the woman's apartment and everything is immaculate. Everything is in place. When she gives you the tour of the place you have to laugh at her bedroom. Her bed is an altar. You know this is not the place for you. You pull yourself out of the hat. It's the first trick you master as you decide to become an elder.

There is that moment when a man moves beyond desire. When he no longer needs to turn around to look at a woman. Months before working on this book I stopped drinking beer and wine. Funny how I no longer have the taste or even the craving for it. Magic? How did I make the thirst disappear? Was it discipline or just the ability to finally understand the game?

How does a coach or manager know where to place his players on the field? Move the centerfielder over a few steps. Tell the third baseman to play back at third. Swing the shortstop over behind the bag. Look into a woman's eye or listen to her voice and you'll see she's trying to get to first. Be too sweet and she'll steal second and your money. It was Denise who once called me a fool to my face. I was sending an old girlfriend money in California. This was before the invention of the internet and those scam letters from Nigeria.

I was once a sucker for breasts, butts, and brains. Now that I'm no longer drinking I can see the drinks I had were very weak. I know how to call my own game but I worry about my son. Did Houdini have headaches? Is it all done by having faith in mirrors? A father looks at a son. The son looks at his father. It's just a mirror. I tell my son to never mistake grace for salvation. I made that mistake once. So did our nation.

I was talking to my sister when I was outlining this book. I was curious about the things she remembered and how they affected her. I asked her about the assassination of John Kennedy. She sent me the following email:

It had only been a few months since I entered nursing school. I was just beginning life on my own with new living quarters, new freedoms, new friends and responsibilities. I was about to take a pharmacology test when the teacher rushed in and told us the president had been shot. Some people like me were stunned into silence; others started crying, some just gasped "no."

Many students, myself included, rushed to the nearby church to pray. When we returned to the classroom we were told the president was dead. Suddenly everything was gray and for the next few days I just moved very slowly. I stayed glued to the TV watching the president being shot over and over again, trying to make sense of what was on the screen. I guess my feelings were "what

101

next?" When things get this bad surely something else is just around the corner.

I need to know what's around the corner. I need to know how many innings I have. How many pages? I could stop here. But what would you know about my life? Do you want another turn at bat? Another swing?

As I get older the poems appear less and less. The personal is prose. I feel comfortable fathering words. If I could draw (again), I would purchase sketch pads and pens that possessed their own minds. Still life. Should I do a self-portrait? Begin with the eyes? They are tired and look like my brother's when he was in his thirties and working at Bankers Trust. I have no idea what his job was. My mother said he made good money and that was all that mattered. How do you go from a monastery to a bank without getting lost? If I could find words, I would retrace my brother's journey. Who did he turn to for advice and guidance? Maybe he is saying his prayers and preparing for bed. In his hands, a letter from my mother. She hints about how difficult it is for his father to pay so many bills. She has no words to say she misses him. It's impossible to say more than one word at once. Her mouth a flood of words, and then the levee breaks. He is crying and decides to return home. Who does he tell? He tells no one. One day he gets out of a cab on Westchester Avenue in the Bronx. He carries his one suitcase up the hill. The projects have not changed. He waits for the one working elevator to take him up to the 7th floor.

He rings the door bell. He rings it again. He wakes my father who slowly leaves his bed, slowly walks to the door and slowly opens it. My brother looks into our father's eyes and quickly they embrace. My father is crying. He rubs my brother's bald head. He rubs it again. He rubs it again. He rubs it again. He takes the suitcase out of my brother's hand. He closes the door. It's just my brother and father looking at one another. "You look good," they both say at the same time.

Was it my mother who first understood the power of words? Did she know that a letter added to a letter added to a letter added to a letter – was power? What stories did she tell to convince my brother to return home? What stories did she tell that confused his own? The stories were never true. Did my mother throw her first born a curve?

I can't make any sense out of my brother's life. Is this why my own is still a mystery? I wrote once about my mother wanting to give me away at birth. What proof do I have? Is this where my pain begins? Rejected? Given away? Not wanted? How many times did my mother often forget my name? How many times did she call me Richard? How many times did she call me a mystery?

I seem to have my control back. Stab at the rubber – once, now twice. I should try and talk to my mother again. Maybe we can begin by talking about the weather. Is it going to rain?

Sitting at the small table in her apartment on Chambers Street, my mother is eating Chinese food. It's almost a ritual we have when I make a trip north to New York. In between the shrimp fried rice, beef with onions, and egg rolls, we small talk. I'm company and not really a son. I'm not the television or the radio that keeps her company. I am company. My mother wants to serve the food. There is only one question she will keep asking again and again. "Do you have enough?" "Do you have enough?" My mother's life has always revolved around serving food to someone. Night after night she rose from bed to fix my father a meal when he came home in the early morning hours.

A good marriage is a good meal. It's the food that turns cold long before the sex and love. "Do you have enough?" "Do you have enough?"

IN SPORTS YOU EARN your nickname. I became
Ethelbert sitting in a Howard dorm trying to come up
with a campaign slogan so I could be elected freshman
class treasurer. Who has the job of giving names to hur-
ricanes and storms? Did I meet Katrina before she met
New Orleans?

There are things you can't remember and there
are things you can't forget. I forget names just a few minutes after an introduction. I can't forget Katrina. I went
down to New Orleans several months after the destruc-
tion. I didn't know what to expect or what I would see. I
was invited by one of the public libraries to give a talk
on Langston Hughes. I've known rivers but I've never
known a levee when it broke. Months after Katrina (and
Rita) I walked off an airplane into the New Orleans hu-
midity and heat. Like a Louis Armstrong trumpet blast
I could immediately smell the musk from the carpet in
the terminal. Was this the same place where I saw se-
nior citizens packed next to one another in the baggage
claim area? After the rain, after the flood, it was the
elderly that left me with the most haunting images.

You live your entire life and this is how you suffer in your seventies, eighties, and nineties? Your head titling down as you sit in a wheelchair. Your arm outstretched begging for a cool drink of water.

I thought of old people when I thought of Katrina. I thought of my mother being able to survive 9/11 but not Katrina. You can't get your medicine. You're diabetic and you can't walk and you can barely see. You wait for the government as if Lincoln was still president. It's almost Juneteenth before FEMA has an excuse for their failure.

When I reconnect with some of my friends who live in New Orleans, there isn't much to say. Some survived but lost everything or maybe some things. Kalamu ya Salaam his tapes and recordings, Jerry Ward his Richard Wright books and notes. Mona Lisa Saloy her space. But New Orleans is first always Brenda Marie Osbey for me; as years ago it was Tom Dent. Brenda Marie the poet, the poet laureate. The woman whose beauty and words are as enchanting as the city's history. Osbey. You say her name and it seems to convey the image of a remote. Pass the Osbey. Where is the Osbey? Click. Click. You call her and learn that she is well, and so is her mother. When I finally visit New Orleans months later after Katrina, it's Brenda Marie who takes me around the French Quarter like some angel checking on the spirits. One morning we sit in her favorite cafe, laughing as if Baldwin or someone was late. It's times like these that are so few and special that I don't even want to write them down. You think about the fire next time and you're not afraid of the fire but rather the ashes.

I've known many writers during my life, but the special moments can be counted on just one hand. The moment when hearts touch hearts. The moment when friendship becomes a much deeper bond than sex. In Seattle I sit by a lake with Zoe Anglesey and we look at the water. In Bennington, Reetika Vazirani and I sit on a bench with our backs and heads touching. "I can feel where your poems come from," I joke.

Katrina wore black. Zoe and Reetika both dead. How high the water, how deep the pain? How many of us are survivors? My father and brother also gone ahead. Higher ground. From the mound I count my blessings. This memoir could be a sermon on the Mount. Katrina made me think about the constant danger that surrounds us. A change in the weather can change anyone's life. Katrina could be that other woman who turns your life upside down. You remember her name was Stephanie. You remember Denise pulling you out of the water before you drowned. For years you debated the role of marriage and government. As you get older you keep wondering why did your ass fall in the water again?

Some folks have moved back to New Orleans, others never will. Rebuilding means a belief in extra innings. Right now I only believe in five. I wonder what Denise believes in? She came back from visiting her parents in Iowa and mentioned how old they had become. Denise looks into the mirror at her own graying hair – how much of the gray has been my fault? Is stress the silent killer or is it the silent husband? You move around silently in a house of silence. When you go out to eat at a restaurant, you select the silent table by the wall. You listen to the sound food makes in each other's mouths. The only thing worse is eating alone.

I need to call my mother and see if she just ordered Chinese food. I wonder what her nickname was when she was young?

ANOTHER E-NOTE: August 31, 2005

I received this note from the poet Brenda Marie Osbey:

Dear Ethelbert,

Thanks for checking in with me. I'm fine. James drove my Mother and me out on Sunday afternoon. After much tooling about Arkansas and Mississippi, we've settled for now in Shreveport, LA, at the Isle of Capri Casino Hotel. Don't have a laptop or notebook computer, just hotel business center access. Have no idea where we'll head from here. Brought only a couple of days worth of stuff. Thanks so much for looking out for me. Tell everybody I'm out and okay. Will try to keep in touch, love.

Brenda-Marie.

Very sad to see the developments in New Orleans and parts of Mississippi. I've been trying to get in touch with friends. This is when the blues singer stands on a hill and simply wails and sings about the ways things are lost and gone. Levees breaking and the dead can't swim no more. A woman on a roof and not a man in sight.

I'm thinking about Brenda Marie, Jerry W, Kalamu, Mona Lisa, and so many others. Life, homes, and possessions...

SOME PEOPLE FIND BASEBALL slow and boring. Guys standing around in the field, waiting for the next play. A guy pacing in the dugout, spitting, looking at the scoreboard. Relief pitchers in the bullpen talking to fans, eating sunflower seeds, resting their arms. A batter in the on-deck circle gripping his bat, weighing the number of hits in it. An infielder poking in the dirt like a chicken, marking the place that he knows is his. Time stops. Anticipation. A great catch? Strikeout? Double play? Hit and Run? A Buddhist might call it samsara. Nothing but wandering during those moments between pitches.

I think of people homeless from wars, natural disasters, and doing nothing but waiting. I think of how a person wanders throughout life looking for purpose, direction, and meaning. If you're an artist, you wait for that painting, song, or poem to pull you aside and let you know the waiting is over. Maybe it comes after the first book, maybe the second. Maybe it never comes and you're in twilight time waiting for the miracle and it's not going to happen. If baseball is slow, then life is fast. It doesn't go backwards, only forward into the unknown. Faith is the only guarantee that there will always be a third out.

When June Jordan was fighting illness, I remember her taking a pile of pills. A line of pills on the table. A foul line. An indication that you're on the other side of your health. Pills keeping you in the game. Pills moving the pain into the corner and giving you another chance to catch your breath. Yes, breath. This is what keeps you going. Breath. Stop and pay attention to the air going in and out of your lungs. Breathe. Think of the moment. Mindfulness.

On my table right now there is just one pill. I will be able to measure my decline by how many more pills I place on the table. Playing the colors and size is what I'll be doing if I make it into the sixth and seventh innings.

In the fifth inning the pitching coach looks at this cliffboard and counts the number of balls and strikes. How many chapters do I have in me? A friend who is an agent tells me she can't sell anything that's under 75,000 words. I push the idea of publishing out of my mind. It's a distraction. Why does a person become a writer? I'm back to trying to answer this question again. I think I started keeping a blog because I had no one to talk to. I also felt no one listened to what I was saying half the time. I'm writing for future readers now. Fans who will look at the record books and conclude that I attempted to live a decent life. Shoeless Joe Jackson? Black Arts Movement or Black Sox Scandal? Ethelbert, a shoeless son-of-a-gun lacking a second college degree and almost every book written out of print.

Etta James singing "This Bitter Earth" over and over again as I brush the gray in my hair.

> *This bitter earth*
> *Can it be so cold*
> *Today you're young*
> *Too soon you're old*

I stop to breathe and catch my breath. The one pill I'm taking is for hypertension. High blood pressure. Check the milligrams. Millergrams? How do I measure my life? Here is a list of the things I cannot do:

Drive a car
Ride a bike
Skate
Bowl
Dance
Repair things
Assemble things
Dribble a basketball
Do math in my head
Understand taxes
Take my blood pressure

When did these problems begin? Is the above just a list poem trying to slip into this prose? Change one thing on the list and my life would be different. Maybe the loneliness could have been pushed aside by jumping into a car and driving somewhere. Maybe I could have offered someone a ride instead of always being driven. Driven. Driven. Driven. All my life. Driven. Driven. Driven. Waiting to be driven. Waiting for the driver. Waiting to be picked up. Waiting to be taken home? Driven home. Driven out of my mind. Crazy now. Maybe if I could dance I would not be Crazy Legs making a fool of myself on a dance floor. That happened once in a dorm at Howard and I never danced again. I was having fun until someone asked me what the hell I was doing. Was the music just in my head? What were other people listening too? Is this why I'm always without a partner? If I could ride a bike, would I have a bike partner? So many people taking their bikes out together. Bike. Hike. I'm the person left behind to wander alone. When things break look for someone else to fix it. When I break there is no one here to fix it.

My father and brother, two broken men. I see the pieces of their lives in my memory. Even trying to write about them, trying to lift their lives up into stories, cuts my hands. Is this the curse of blood? Is this why I've been bleeding all my life? Did my brother try to hide in a monastery?

The door opens and my father sees my brother standing in the doorway. He's happy but he knows his son has failed in becoming a monk. When he puts his arms around his son, he feels like he is holding himself.

He can't let go. Father and son or blood brothers? There is compassion here but I can't measure it.

> *Inside your glove you hold it and keep waiting*
> *for it to speak. The silence tells its own story.*
> *The game keeps searching for an author.*

I've been stuck at different times while writing this memoir. It's not the typical writing block. It's not finding the words but instead looking at them on the page without crying. I need the strength to continue and the feeling that I'm writing what needs to find its air. Words trying to breathe. How do I free them from my imagination? How can my words speak for the dead? Will this book speak for me after I'm gone? I never thought about this. I did discuss the idea once of speaking for the dead in a memoir workshop. It wasn't a writing exercise but rather an attempt to look beyond one's life. It was also a way of thinking about the responsibilities authors have.

> *The trembling of dreams is everywhere, like the*
> *wind.*
>
> – *Jayanta Mahapatra*

17

What happens to dreams when you reach the middle years and innings? Do you cash in the chips? Do you attempt to dream again? "Act your age," I'm always reminded. You're no longer a kid or a young man. You're as old as everyone's dad. You are a dad and don't forget it! I was sitting in the Mocha Hut on Florida Avenue (not far from Howard) when I looked around and suddenly realized that I was older than everyone in the place by a good twenty or thirty years. No wonder the conversations were looped.

I look at the names in my cell phone directory, and only 20 people listed are older than me. Where is my team? The only person who is my exact age is Denise. When people are married for a long time they begin to look alike. Denise looks unhappy.

Sometimes she's nice to me and puts her arm around me like Pee Wee Reese. She's independent. If she was a pitcher, she would shake the catcher's signals off again and again. Denise will always throw the pitch she wants to throw. It doesn't matter what the situation is. I'm looking around and the bases are loaded. What do I do now? I look around the Mocha Hut and it's a good indication of how bad the pitching is these days. If I left Denise, where would I go?

My father would never turn his back on his family. My father went to work more than Cal Ripken. He did his duty. My father fell in love while the country still had a draft. He enlisted with Enid, my mother. His tour of duty received few medals and fewer thanks. For much of my childhood my father was simply there. He slept, ate, watched television, and went to work. If he had a few days off in the summer he enjoyed going to the beach. My father couldn't swim – something I can't do either. I should go back a page or two and add swimming to the list.

Denise loves water. A day before her birthday she drives down to Virginia Beach by herself. It's become a ritual. I can see her saying prayers near the ocean. She speaks to God in that Black woman voice, "Lord, give me strength to continue." I'm Denise's burden and luggage. I'm the bag she has to drag up and down the stairs. The bag she wished she hadn't packed. On a flight to England, she lost a bag. She was deeply upset. She looked at me as if I had lost it. The flight over the Atlantic was another Middle Passage and I hadn't even reached middle-age yet. If I had looked outside the airplane window, I would have seen nothing but air. "No, I don't know what happened to your bag." I don't know what happened to us on Underwood Street. Which brings me back to this memoir and its search for the narrative. Denise needs to be in the center of this story. In *Fathering Words* I created my sister's voice to help explain my childhood. No way Denise will let me pull words from her mouth. I don't know her. She has to write her own story. "Leave me out of your books the way you left me out of your life," she demands. So now where do I go from here? Chaos or community? Yes, my wife's maiden name was King.

It was Martin Luther King Jr. in his final year that instructed us to believe in the Beloved Community. How do we learn to commit ourselves to a world of lasting compassion and peace? St. John the Apostle, the founder of the Community of the Beloved Disciple, told us how to live our lives after the resurrection and ascension of Jesus. How do we reunite the feminine and masculine aspects of Christ? Divine revelation as a personal experience.

When my brother died, he left me an envelope with a blank black sheet of paper inside. A Zen koan? Nothing but a riddle for me to think about every day? What about all those things that were in a suitcase given to me after his funeral? What did my brother leave behind? Inside his suitcase nothing but books and notes dealing with the teachings of St. John. How many years did it have to take for me to finally understand my brother's life? A man could spend half his life trying to extract meaning from a black sheet of paper. Maybe it was nothing but a black sheet of paper. All the time the "answers" were in the suitcase. When a man has to travel, he has to pack, even if the only thing he plans to take or carry is himself.

Oh, and the suitcase? What does it look like? It reminds me so much of the type an immigrant would arrive with. Could this have been something my father gave to my brother? Did someone give it to him as a gift? Did it make him feel like he was walking in my father's shoes? In my Underwood home my brother's suitcase is in the basement. My cat used to sleep on it and perhaps dreamt Egyptian dreams. My son told me a story once of how he hid in the basement because he didn't want to go to school. He said he tried to climb into one of the suitcases kept in the basement. Was it the one that belonged to his uncle? Is my son Houdini? Can he climb into a suitcase and escape?

Sometimes I wish I could disappear, but I'm not a magician. My son said he once looked at me with wonder. Maybe he believes in magic.

I wonder when my daughter will get married. I can see myself escorting her to the alter and into the arms of her husband. What did I teach my daughter about marriage? I remember the many conversations and disagreements we had about affirmative action, reparations, the Middle East, Hillary Clinton, journalism, law school, and the Lakers. I think she was hurt when Kobe was caught for letting a woman walk into his Colorado hotel room. You grow up having sports heroes and then they disappoint you. So many New York Yankee players refused to sign my glove when I waited outside the ballpark. Was that me with Carlton,

Patrick, Eddie – The St. Mary's crew? I should have invented friendship after moving out of the projects.

Ball four. It was the young Jim Bouton who was the nicest baseball player I've ever met. I got his autograph around the time he was pitching hard and his cap kept falling off. What's the difference between signing a glove or a book? I might have been by myself that day. Or maybe that was the day Carlton got sick and vomited over everyone on line going to the game.

My daughter did the same thing when she was a baby. Denise and I went to see Ahmad Jamal at Carter Baron. Jasmine-Simone was still at that bottle milk stage. A hot night. Jasmine took her solo right before the jazz band came on. She played a warm milk stench that quickly rode the air and covered about four rows. Nothing Denise and I could do but rise and go look for the parked car. We looked over our shoulders like helicopters bypassing the 9th Ward in New Orleans.

When writing the memoir the mind has a tendency to cut and paste. So my childhood overlaps with my daughter's. Jasmine-Simone – my first child. I treat her the way my father treated my brother. You want to lift the first child into your arms, swing her around, make funny faces, and do crazy dances to make her laugh.

My daughter becomes my partner but it's only a matter of time before someone wants to interrupt the dance. How many women are waiting for their lover's autograph? How many will be disappointed when the ink fades or smears? Ball four. Someone decides to walk.

We live inside the dream that our children's world will be better than the one we inherited.

If I didn't have a memory, I wouldn't know where anything is.

– Phil Schaap

When baseball returned to Washington D.C., I took the Metro over to RFK stadium to watch the Washington Nationals play the Seattle Mariners. Walk into any ballpark and the green grass of the outfield, the four white bases, the stands, the smell of food, the signs, the scoreboard, the kids with gloves, folks wearing jerseys of star players, the sounds of balls jumping off bats, and your seat in the middle of it all waiting for you; this is the reason you were born. The child in you returns and you turn to see if you're in a position to catch a ball. When the National Anthem is played you look out at the Beloved Community.

Ichiro Suzuki is my favorite baseball player. I have no words to describe his play. Perfection in motion? Hit. Run. Catch. Throw. Speed. Grace. In my bedroom closet an Ichiro jersey sent from Seattle by my friend Don Mee Choi. When Ichiro first started playing in America, Don Mee sent me a steady flow of articles. I follow Ichiro's career the way some writers read Joyce. I remember the criticism and doubt expressed by sportswriters about his talent. Too small. He won't make it in the majors. A different type of game in America? What about a different America? I look at my son and daughter and realize it's their time too. Both have defied their critics. The only thing I could ever be is a fan.

The piano ain't got no wrong notes.

– Thelonious Monk

ICHIRO ONLY MADE ONE ERROR in the 2007 baseball season. I find that amazing. Almost perfection.
I remember my son leading his JV basketball team
at Gonzaga (DC) to an undefeated season. The last
game against DeMatha he put a team on his back and
willed them to a championship. In 2008 he would help
Widener University win their second consecutive basketball title.

The winning comes against the odds. After a season I seem to always watch my son being overlooked
at an award ceremony. Once a school gave him a BS
"Unsung Hero" award that we tossed into the trunk of
the car before Denise drove us home. Sometimes after
my son has been disappointed by things in his life, I
start to believe all Miller men might be cursed. It's either believing in the negative or trying to determine if

there's a higher calling we just haven't reached yet. I want my son and daughter to make fewer mistakes in life than I did. I want them to be prepared for what life throws at them.

I still have my own questions I need to answer. My sister gave me a nice black journal to take to VCCA. I've been keeping notes for this memoir in it. I sat down about two days ago to think about questions I needed to ask myself. What do I want to do with the rest of my life? I wrote down the following:

What goals do I have right now?
Zero.

What plans?
Zero.

Retirement? When?
?

Where would I like to be buried?
?

Am I happy?
No.

Why do I feel lonely so often?
No one to talk or hang out with. Absence of a best friend.

Who are the people I correspond with on a regular basis?
Charles Johnson and Julia Galbus.

Do I like my job?
No. Dislike work environment.

Will I ever have a clean and modern office?
A door would be nice.

What type of work do I enjoy?
Radio and televison.

Things I would like to own:
A very good laptop computer.

Things to improve on:
Technological skills.

What would make me feel more secure?
Savings in the bank. Emergency fund.

      The list of questions is far from exhaustive. What should I be doing during the next two years? I'm running out of time just at the moment in which I'm beginning to understand how time functions. I think of old black men sitting in front of store fronts. They wear suits, ties, good shirts, and suspenders. These men are elders. Masons? They are deacons. Race men. They play checkers and sit down with the wind. I've been wasting a lot of time. I could be reading more and perhaps earning more. I had the goal of finishing this memoir before Denise returned to VCCA to pick me up. It seems possible. Earlier today I printed out what I had written.

This memoir has a jazz feel to it. Is it BeBop? Parker and Diz? I like the energy that flows from one short chapter into another. Balls and strikes. No wild pitches so far. Right here I stop and play *The Gentle Side of John Coltrane*, you know where he does that Billy Eckstine tune, "I Want To Talk About You."

My daughter wears her hair short like her mother. I always knew she would. On the eve of graduating from law school, I can see her entering the political arena and fighting for change. Jasmine-Simone is also a marathon runner and maybe this skill will help her work for social change and dig in for the long haul. My daughter is Lou Brock. I remember visiting her in Boston one summer. She had an internship doing some legal housing work with a program run by Harvard. When she showed me her one-room basement apartment I wanted to weep. The place was something that might have inspired a Russian novelist before the revolution. Was my daughter now the protagonist in Ellison's novel? I looked at the ceiling expecting to see more than one light bulb. Here was another moment of failure in my life. My father would never have let Marie stay in a place like this. My daughter was in this situation because of how much I had in my pocket. In my fifties and I'm still saving pennies and looking for quarters that might have rolled under the bed. I was in the supermarket last year. The guy in front of me had just cashed his paycheck. He had bills in his hand and he was buying things for his child's birthday. He went to give the clerk some cash and she told him to wait. She hadn't added the price of the cake to his bill. "Oh, man, I hate to part with my money," he said. I joked with the guy and reminded him that he didn't have candles for the cake. "Oh, man, that's the first thing I put back," he replied. I walk out of my daughter's Boston apartment and an old song by The Four Tops leaves a scratch on my back. I want to know "who left the cake out in the rain?"

My wife is Curt Flood. Denise changed me before I knew I was changing. She was the person always reminding me that Howard University was paying me what folks made in the old Negro League. Where would Jackie Robinson be without Rachel?

E-Note: May 3, 2008

Buzzie Bavasi dead at 93.
I always loved this guy's name. I loved reading the following in his Washington Post *obit:*

In 1946, when Brooklyn's general manager, Branch Rickey, was contemplating bringing Jackie Robinson to the Dodgers as the major leagues' first African American player, he asked Mr. Bavasi to learn more about Robinson's character.

Among other things, Mr. Bavasi traveled to Montreal, where Robinson was playing with the Dodgers' Triple A franchise. He sat behind the wives section and was as impressed by Robinson's wife, Rachel, as by anything he saw on the baseball diamond.

"I told Mr. Rickey that if Jackie is good enough for Rachel, he's good enough for the Dodgers," Mr. Bavasi said years later.

- posted by Ethelbert Miller @ 6:59 A.M.

Flood and I can't swim. Another thing to add to that list of things I can't do. Denise drops my hand as we cross a street in Silver Spring, Maryland. Why hold hands if you can't drive? I must be on the dark side of the road. Dylan reminding me to "Don't Think Twice." Denise wondering if she has given me her heart or her soul. We are survivors. I think of this word and how haunting it has been to use or repeat. I once wrote an essay in a magazine in which I mentioned that my deepest fear was to be a survivor. I don't want to be the person discovered after being underground and trapped for 14 hours. I don't want to be the person lost in the mountains and freezing for days. I'm just a guy in a second marriage. I can't tell if I'm looking at two balls or two strikes. How do we survive? Was it June Jordan who once wrote that we survive love by continuing to love? Do we look for renewal after failure? Is change renewal? When should I give up the ghost? Is every free-agent free?

My son is Bob Gibson. Cardinals link him to men who died before he was born. We sit on the steps outside our home on Underwood Street. Another argument with his mother. "I'm not you," he tells me. Prophetic? Who am I? Denise thinks therapy might help. I recall my father talking to himself and decide it's not a good idea. I look over at my son still angry with how things are going in his young life. He once kicked his basketball out of the park one morning. I went and got it. When I brought it back I yelled in his face, "You don't kick the ball! You never kick the ball! The ball is your friend!" Years later after missing three fouls shot in a row during a championship game with the clock showing just a few seconds left – he would remember my words. One never knows what a child will remember. One never knows what a wife might not forget. Is the ball still my friend? Where is the park? My son and I put our arms around each other and go back inside. Did Bob Gibson ever apologize for throwing a hard fast one near a batter's head? Yeah, the ball was his friend.

FLORIDA IS WHERE MANY baseball teams have their spring training camps. A couple of my cousins went to live there after retirement. My cousin Ken Elam lives near Orlando. A few months before writing this book, I was in the state doing a site visit of the Florida State Humanities Council in St. Petersburg. Ken drove over and then drove me back to his home. I teased him about living in Shaq's house when I walked through the front door. Ken's father was a good friend to my father. Two guys falling in love with the Marshall girls. Enid was my father's girlfriend. Ken's father fell for Evelyn.

Talking to Ken about old times is like being up in the sports booth. The game looks different and makes better sense just before it goes into the official record book. I guess here is where folks call the errors they see on the field. It's just Ken and me talking and eating Chinese food. A family tradition? Ken no longer needs to read the fortune cookie. He has done well. He did what the men in our family have always done. He has worked at one job and retired. Cal Ripken? Joe DiMaggio? Jackie? This is what many of the old guys did. Willie Mays was a fool to put on a New York Mets uniform. Poor Roger Clemens might be buried naked.

It's from Ken that I get another picture of my father. It's like now I have a baseball card to go with the memories. Into the night and another day, Ken and I talk about fatherhood and how to raise children. He is separated from his son's mother who lives in New Jersey – so the goodnight kisses must be made over the phone. Ken seems to talk to his son every day. I can count the number of telephone conversations I had with my own father. I could try to multiply them and still come away with a single digit.

Spring training and suddenly you're old. If luck knows your name, the old baseball team might invite you to the camp to coach and advise the rookies. You might be asked to teach them how to bunt or steal a base. Much of the time you'll stand around in the field feeling the sun on your shoulders, teasing you to believe you can still catch and run with the best. I look over at Ken as he drives me to the Orlando Airport. He seems very happy with the cards of life. Playing card games is another thing I can't do. Add it to the list. I reach into the trunk of Ken's car and grab my luggage. I'm heading north to write a book. The title is going to be *The 5th Inning*. My cousin Ken is going to be in it. On the airplane I open another notebook and make notes.

One of the nicest people at VCCA is Kay Ruane. She is a visual artist and represents a gallery in Boston.

She's the only person I've spoken to in my life who survived an airplane crash. I think about her story as I write this book. She's a survivor. I keep looking at her. I watch her make her lunch in the kitchen. She is cutting fruit and placing everything nicely in a bowl. I think she's secretly a magician. How else could she escape a burning plane? I keep feeling trapped in my life. How did she do it? I take more notes. I have one more week left to my residency. It's not about fathering more words. It's about living and finding a new reason to live.

The last game of baseball I played was at Bennington. Softball. Poets against fiction writers. I was out in left field. In the second inning, a ball was hit my way. You misjudge things when you're either young or old. I was surprised when the ball landed in my glove. Third out. I trotted off the field in my old gait. Did I still have it? I have to bat this inning. After swinging at two pitches and tipping both of them, I tap a slow roller back to the mound. The pitcher is a core faculty member in the Writing Seminars. As I run to first base my legs remind me that they are all I have left. I'm safe and there is another runner on third base. A few batters later and the game is dinner conversation along with prose poems.

There was one memorable softball game where Liam was pitching and running the bases. We thought it would be the day of his heart attack. It was the day Joyce Maynard got a hit and someone stuck her in right field where she held her glove as beautiful as Roberto Clemente. It was seeing the fun on Joyce's face that gave me the idea of funding the game on a regular basis. The Miller Classic. An annual event at the Bennington Writing Seminars heading into its third year as I write this memoir. With the money I contribute, the winners are able to purchase books of poetry from the college bookstore.

We need baseball in our lives. We need our fields of dreams. The game is played between the lines. Even when we fail our actions go into the record book.

If we become stars or legends, we make it to the Hall of Fame. Our numbers will be retired. 42 forever. Jackie Robinson's number.

I look around at all the new inventions and gadgets and slowly recognize that my time on this earth is almost over. Some things I will never learn how to operate. I'm old-fashioned and maybe the only thing that might survive from the old game is the scoreboard in Fenway Park. Where have you gone Pumpsie Green?

I have only returned once to my brother and father's upstate New York gravesite. My sister makes the trip regularly since she lives in nearby Yonkers. I prefer to tell the stories of their lives. I will continue to do this until I surrender to air. It's the only way I can make sense out of my own life. The more I remember and discover about these men, the bluer their lives become. Instead of writing books, I should be making maps. Ethelbert as cartographer. Where is the known world?

Sometimes I'm the shortstop who forgets to touch second base during a double play. There are things an umpire never sees.

"Honey, I'll come and get you," Denise says in the middle of our conversation. In a few days, I'll pack my clothes, books, cds, and this manuscript that one day might become a book. It's not a big book. It's only five innings.

THE KNUCKLEBALL OR KNUCKLER IS erratic and unpredictable. Erratic? Is that what the E stands for? I thought this memoir was going to end with the last chapter. On September 20, 1958, in the drizzle, Hoyt Wilhelm of the Baltimore Orioles threw a no-hitter against the New York Yankees. By coincidence the opposing pitcher was Don Larsen who had thrown his no-hitter two years before in the World Series. Wilhelm was perhaps the greatest knuckleballer to play the game. Known mostly as a relief pitcher, when he started the game against the Yankees his record was 2-10. I wonder what my record is as I write this book? 2-10?

I wonder what Denise thinks my record is? All these years married to a guy with poor stats. Erratic. A guy who never seems happy, always complaining. She instructs me to stop moaning and do something with my life. She looks at other writers on television and everyone else seems to be at the Harlem Renaissance. Folks call me for book blurbs, information, suggestions, advice, and contacts. Once I was in the hospital and a guy called about his manuscript. He didn't even inquire how I was doing. If I named names, too many people would take it personally.

I'm starting to think about my final pitch. Maybe walking away from the game and beginning a new life. I think of Jim Bouton, his fastball gone and how he made a comeback with the knuckler. Jim Bouton taking my baseball glove in front of Yankee Stadium and writing his name on it.

I want to be unpredictable if I can't be magical. My friend Charles Johnson nicknamed me the Wizard. In baseball that was Ozzie Smith, making the difficult play look easy. What are the difficult decisions I need to make right now? I've spoken and written so much about love, I need to begin to love myself – my aloneness. Turn the deep blues inside out. Let the air out of the tragedy. After 9/11 people ran home and hugged the people they loved. Why didn't I? Was I a knucklehead?

Every person looks for a grace period in their life. But what if you were to meet Grace? What would she look like? You take note of where you are. You're spinning like a knuckler and becoming more and more erratic. Amazing Grace, how sweet the sound, but only a musician can live on sound. Sirens tell you there is no future unless you return home. You say grace while peeking into your empty hands.

The 5th Inning

You're gonna have to serve somebody,
Well, it may be the devil or it may be the Lord
But you're gonna have to serve somebody.

– Bob Dylan

Wilhelm was a great reliever. The reliever is the person who slams the door. He is the sheriff of victory. Just throw strikes until they take the ball. Behind you are your son and daughter. If you were Paige, you could tell them to sit down on the field. That's how much confidence you had in your arm, your God-blessed talents and skill. Or maybe you were Cool Papa Bell, so fast that you were under the covers before someone turned out the lights.

When my children were younger we would race down the streets. Once leaving Vertigo Bookstore on Connecticut Avenue we ran for the bus. I pulled both hamstrings as my legs turned into busted rubber bands. It was a reminder that I was a dad and not a kid anymore. I dragged my legs to the back of the bus and sat down. I looked into the eyes of Jasmine and Nyere. My two loves. I felt the pain in my legs again. I was 2-10, but ready to throw a no-hitter.

Faith is the substance of things not seen, and hope for things to come.

–Hebrews 11.1

I SEND DENISE AN EMAIL from VCCA. We talk about our children and our love. We count our blessings. I count the days until she comes to take me back to Washington. This afternoon I walked into the library and found an old issue of *The Sun*. I sat down and read a fascinating article about zoos written by Derrick Jensen. His first paragraph made me think of what I was writing. My life?

The bear takes seven steps, her claws clicking on concrete. She dips her head, turns, and walks toward the front of the cage. Another dip, another turn, another three steps. When she gets back to where she started, she begins all over. This is what's left of her life.

Too many of us confine ourselves to boxes and cages. Even if the sky is gray, refuse to give into the darkness. It's been overcast and raining in my fifth inning.Denise and I have no intention of stopping the game. I've pitched myself into trouble and now I have to pitch myself out of it.

Balls and strikes. I'm finally learning how to pitch and not simply throw. A major adjustment that one might call wisdom. I'm becoming an elder and this is where I catch my breath or walk around the mound and kick the dirt, smooth out a place where my feet will land. Life is only a game if you're a child soldier walking around with a gun. It's a game if you're high on drugs. Life is what doesn't show up in the scorecard. It's all those days my father went to work and my brother said his prayers. It's those days when I wondered how I was going to pay another bill. It's my sister taking care of our elderly Mom. It's Denise trying to make the grass grow in the front of our house.

The one baseball record I still find amazing is the one set by Joe DiMaggio. He hit safely in 56 consecutive games, from May 15–July 16, 1941. After his streak was stopped he started a new one and hit in 17 consecutive games. There is no way I will accomplish anything close to this in my life. I'll always be a Ken Keltner type of guy.

As I wait for Denise to arrive, I remember something my friend Suheir Hammad once wrote:

may you walk ever
loved and in love
know the sun
for warmth the moon
for direction

may these words always
remind you   your breath
is sacred   words
bring out
the god in you

He can only hold her for so long
No one's home but the lights are on

     — Amy Winehouse

KIRSTEN PORTER WHO EDITED THIS manuscript wants to discuss the last chapter. She feels I can do better. Maybe she's right. Maybe I'm wrong. What do you think? Every reader is an umpire. Can you tell the difference between balls and strikes?

    Baseball Got Me Outta That Celery Field

       — Buck O'Neal

Baseball is all I know.

         E. Ethelbert Miller
         VCCA
         Amherst, Virginia
         May 18, 2008

They may not have thrown the worst at you yet, but so far you've caught all their pitches.

– Reynolds Price

THE 6TH INNING
(for Michael Mariani)

This is rally time
If you're behind in life.

It's clutch time
If you're serious about relationships.

It's the inning
Before the late ones arrive.

Play hard!
Build a lead and keep it.

Make the beautiful catch
Reporters write about after the game.

Whatever the score
Believe you can win.

Life continues after the 5th.
Love is what you play for.

Tip your cap to the fans.
All dreams can be won.

Always know the score.
Run even when you walk.

Busboys and Poets Press is a subsidiary of Busboys and Poets, a restaurant and community resource center for artists, activists, writers, thinkers, and dreamers who believe that a better world is possible.

Busboys and Poets
2121 14th St. NW
Washington, DC 20009
www.busboysandpoets.com

PM Press was founded at the end of 2007 by a small collection of folks with decades of publishing, media, and organizing experience. PM Press co-conspirators have published and distributed hundreds of books, pamphlets, CDs, and DVDs. Members of PM have founded enduring book fairs, spearheaded victorious tenant organizing campaigns, and worked closely with bookstores, academic conferences, and even rock bands to deliver political and challenging ideas to all walks of life. We're old enough to know what we're doing and young enough to know what's at stake.

We seek to create radical and stimulating fiction and non-fiction books, pamphlets, t-shirts, visual and audio materials to entertain, educate and inspire you. We aim to distribute these through every available channel with every available technology—whether that means you are seeing anarchist classics at our bookfair stalls; reading our latest vegan cookbook at the café; downloading geeky fiction e-books; or digging new music and timely videos from our website.

PM Press is always on the lookout for talented and skilled volunteers, artists, activists and writers to work with. If you have a great idea for a project or can contribute in some way, please get in touch.

PM PRESS
PO Box 23912
Oakland CA 94623
510-658-3906
www.pmpress.org

Also from Busboys and Poets and PM Press

Wisdom Teeth
Derrick Weston Brown, with a foreword by
    Simone Jacobson
978-1-60486-417-5
$14.95

"Full of wit and whimsy, *Wisdom Teeth* postulates a
poetics of heart-whole appreciation and honesty—
for love and life, for family and friends, for literature
and history, for pop culture and the poet's ever-cognizant powers of
observation." —Tony Medina, author of *My Old Man Was Always on
the Lam*

The debut poetry collection from poet and educator Derrick Weston
Brown, *Wisdom Teeth*, is a questioning work, a redefining of personal
relationships, masculinity, race, and history. It's a readjustment of bite,
humor, and perspective as Brown channels hip-hop, Toni Morrison,
and Snagglepuss to make way for the shudder and eruption of wisdom.

Suspended Somewhere Between: A Book of Verse
Akbar Ahmed, with a foreword by Daniel
    Futterman
978-1-60486-485-4
$15.95

"Anyone wanting to understand Islam today must read
Akbar Ahmed's collection." —Greg Mortenson, author of *Three Cups of Tea*

Akbar Ahmed's *Suspended Somewhere Between* is a collection of poetry
from the man the BBC calls "the world's leading authority on contem-
porary Islam." A mosaic of Ahmed's life, which has traversed cultural
and religious barriers, this book of verse is personal with a vocal range
from introspective and reflective to romantic and emotive to historical
and political. The poems take the reader from the forbidding valleys
and mountains of Waziristan in the tribal areas of Pakistan to the think
tanks and halls of power in Washington, DC; from the rustic tranquility
of Cambridge to the urban chaos of Karachi.